Mr. McDoogle Visits The Dinosaurs

Written and Illustrated By:

Marie Whitton

For My Husband
Greg

For My Children
Gregory, Ann-Marie &
Kimberly

For My
Grandchildren

What a beautiful day to take a trip,
Mr. McDoogle will have to zip.
Dinosaurs lived - let's see where,
Let's go there.

Going to the Triassic Period

225 to 200 million years ago

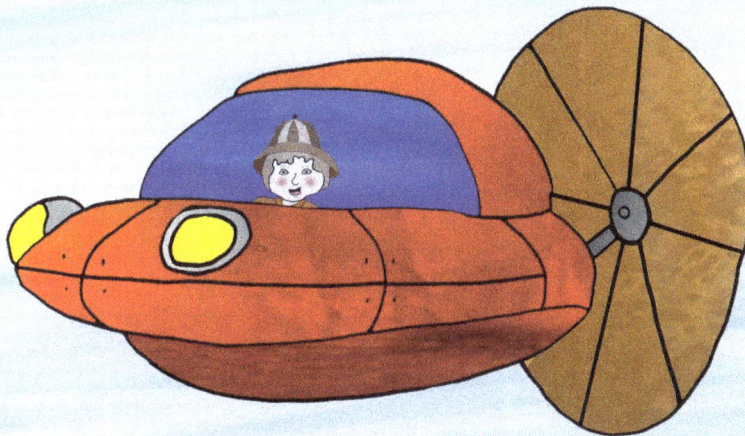

World of the dinosaurs - let's go see,
In Mr. McDoogle's time machine - Wee!
220 million years we go,
Back to the ages of long ago.

A different world - Mr. McDoogle just arrived,
Let's look at how these creatures survived.

Arizonasaurus - a dinosaur - the earth he did roam,
For food - he did comb.
On his back - he has a fin like a sail,
And even a long tail.

Archaeoptery - a pigeon size bird,
The first known bird - this is the word.
With feathers and a beak,
We heard him squeak.

Coelophysis - like a dog - he was small,
Not tall.
Walked on two legs,
And laid about 25 eggs.
They knew they would be snacks,
So they roamed in packs.

Cynognathus - reptile and mammal each half,
Mr. McDoogle started to laugh.
Those teeth - let's look,
His pray - he shook.

Lystrosaurus Mccaig - size of a pig,
He was not big.
Had no teeth - so plants he would eat,
That was his treat.

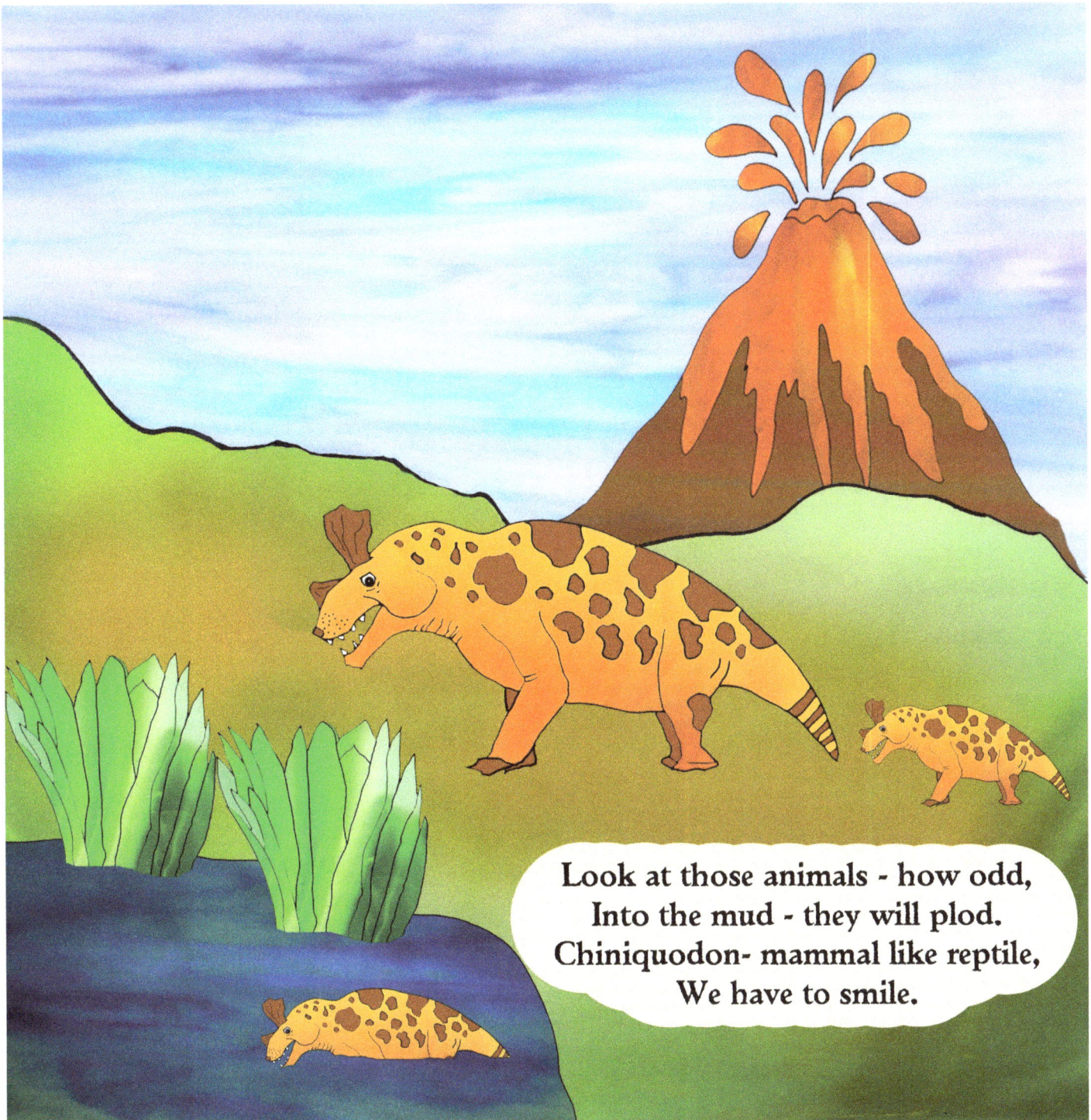

Look at those animals - how odd,
Into the mud - they will plod.
Chiniquodon- mammal like reptile,
We have to smile.

Are there any secrets in this ocean?
It does have a lot of motion.
Mr. McDoogle wants to learn it's history,
So, he will have to dive to find it's mystery.

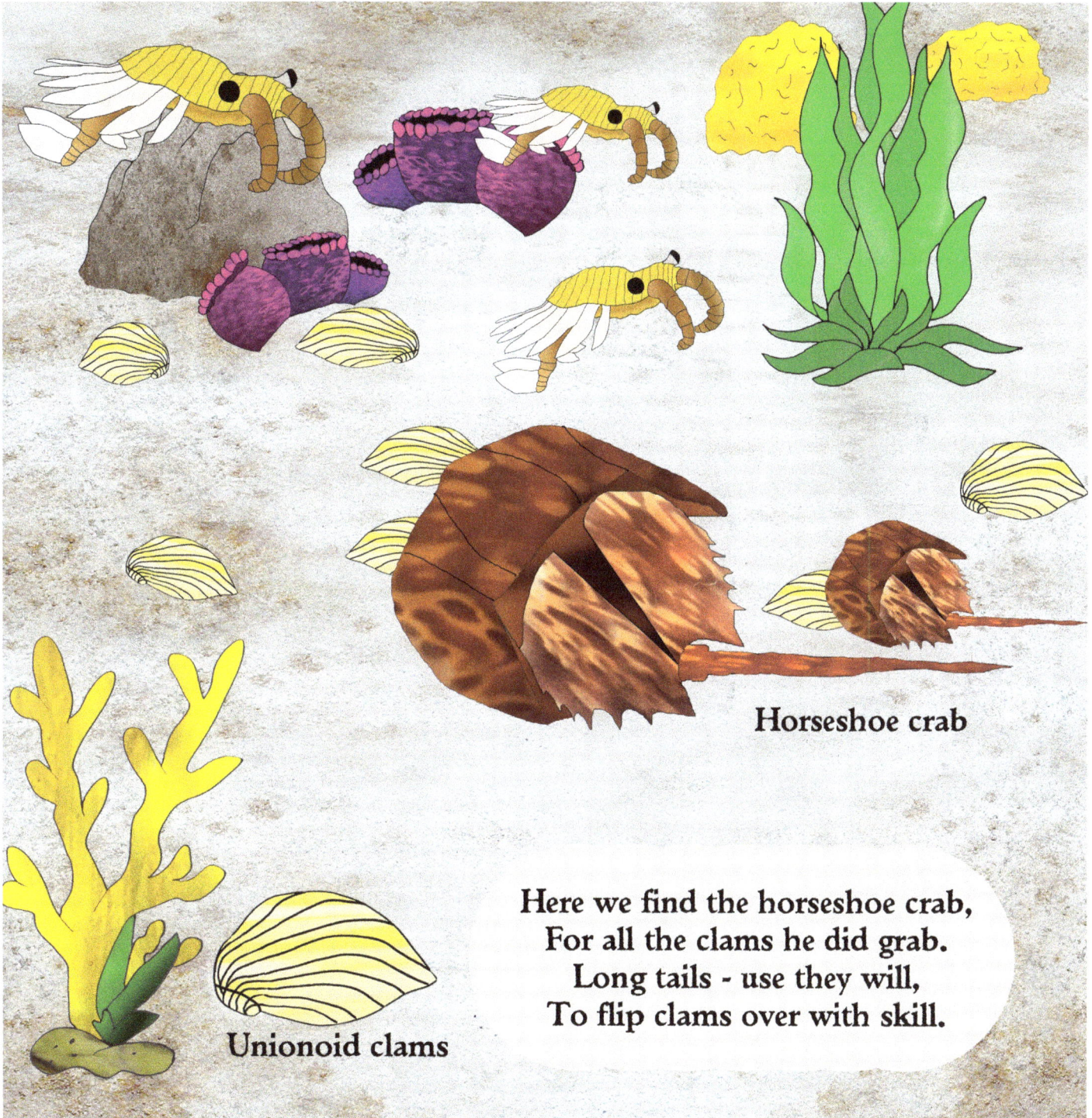

Horseshoe crab

Unionoid clams

Here we find the horseshoe crab,
For all the clams he did grab.
Long tails - use they will,
To flip clams over with skill.

Pliosaurus -
First swimming reptile that is large,
After food he will charge.
Ate fish and squid and snails,
Was the size of five whales.

Ammonites were cousins to the squid,
Inside their shell - they hid.
Up to 3 feet did they grow,
To get away they were not slow.

Nothosaurs - like today's seal,
Ate squid for a meal.
Only grew to 13 feet,
This is neat.

Shark

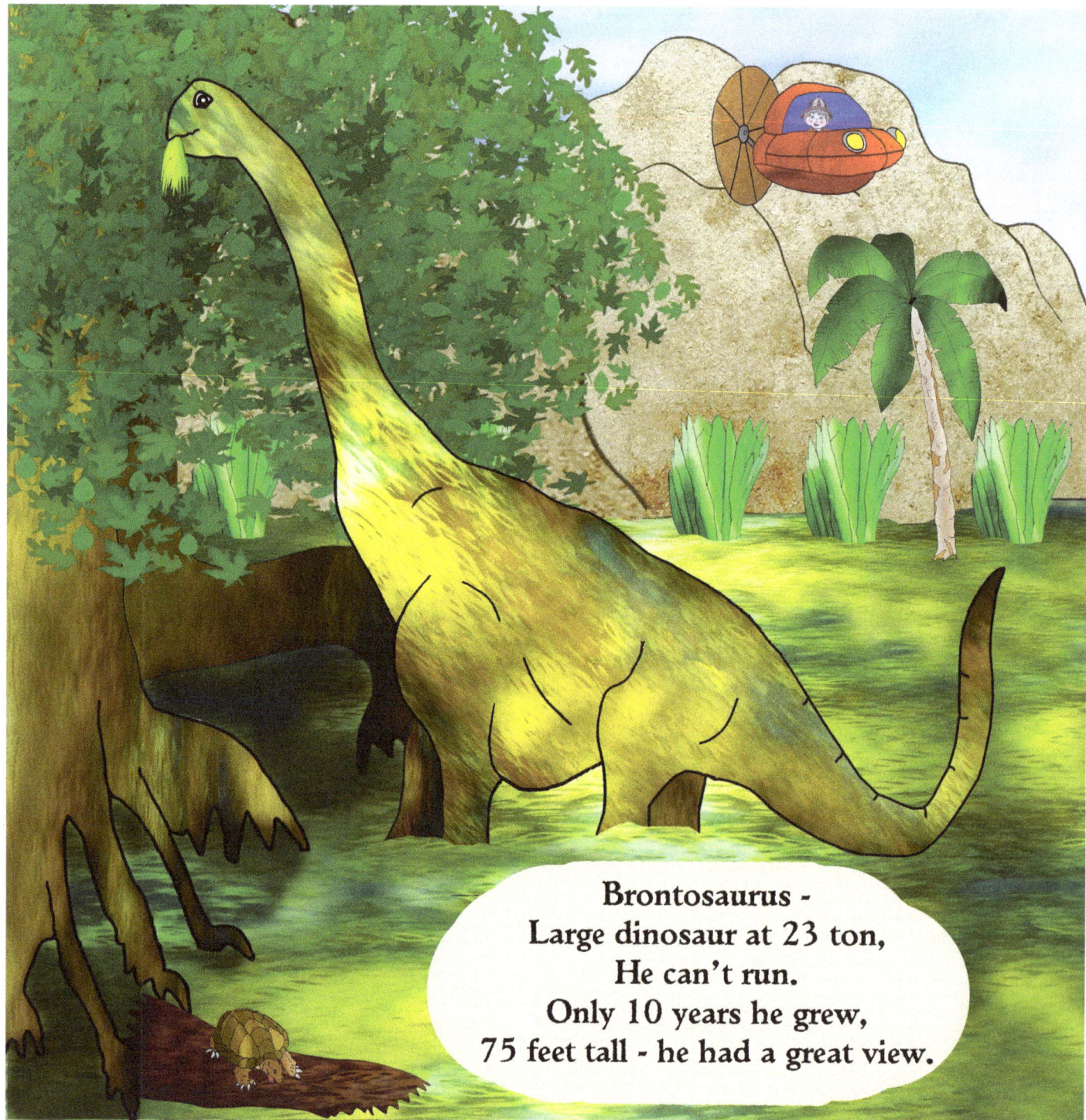

Brontosaurus -
Large dinosaur at 23 ton,
He can't run.
Only 10 years he grew,
75 feet tall - he had a great view.

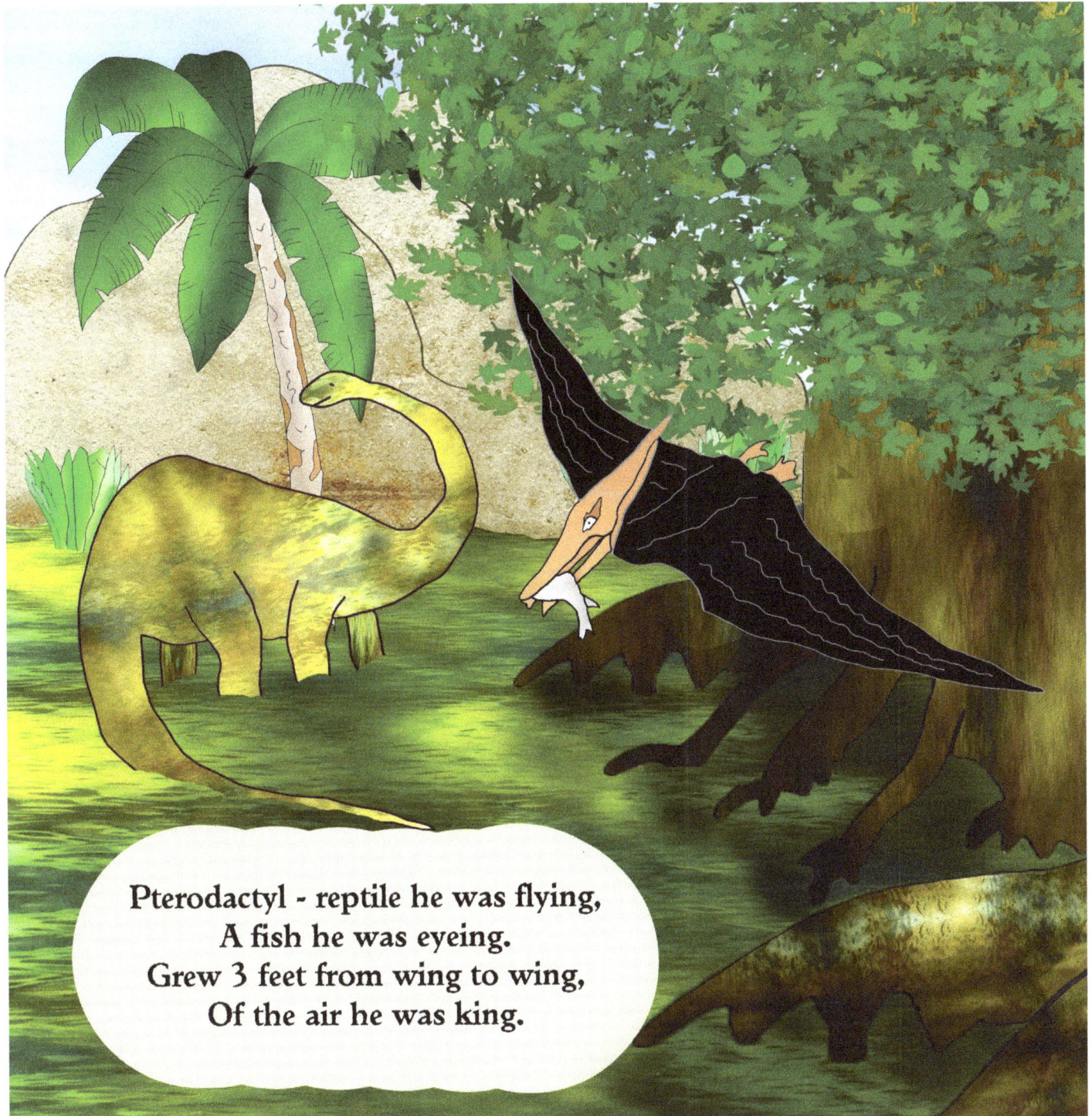

Pterodactyl - reptile he was flying,
A fish he was eyeing.
Grew 3 feet from wing to wing,
Of the air he was king.

Related to Stegosaurus,
Was the Tuojiangosaurus.
Smallest brain of all,
Like a little ball.
4 tons and 23 feet long he was round,
Ate plants from the ground.

Desmatosuchus - cousin to the crocodile and bird,
In the marshy floodplains they lived - we heard.
Weighed 750 pounds and 16 feet long,
He was strong.
Shaped like a shovel was his snoot,
Easy to dig up roots.

Dilophosaurus - a lizard he is,
On his skull he has two ridges that are his.
In a fight - not to fail,
To balance he uses his tail.

Saturnalia - Dinosaur - the oldest known,
This we know from studing it's bone.
Small like a dog - that is the talk,
On two legs - they can walk.

World of the dinosaurs - let's go see,
In Mr. McDoogle's fancy time
machine - Wee!
145 million years we go,
Back to the ages of long ago.

Going to the Jurassic Period

199 to 145 million years ago

Brontosaurus

Look over there at the Brachiosaurus,
Larger than the Brontosaurus.
Wading in the swamp,
Leaves he loves to chomp.

Psephoderma - 10 feet long,
Their jaws were strong.
Loved to eat shell fish,
That was their wish.

Snapping Turtle

Huayangosaurus -
on his back are spikes,
From the spikes the warmth he likes.

Stegosaurus - Let's meet,
Look at that - he is 30 feet.
He walks so very slow,
That we know.
10,000 pounds - he weighs,
All day - on plants he will graze.

Argentinosaurus -
As a turtle he is fast,
Will always come in last.
As large as a football field wide,
At 115 feet long - he can't hide.
Only weighs 85 tons,
Roams around in ones.

Coelurus -
To the bird he is related,
This we stated.
Has a hollow tail,
He is on a food trail.

Archaeoptery

Stenoptery

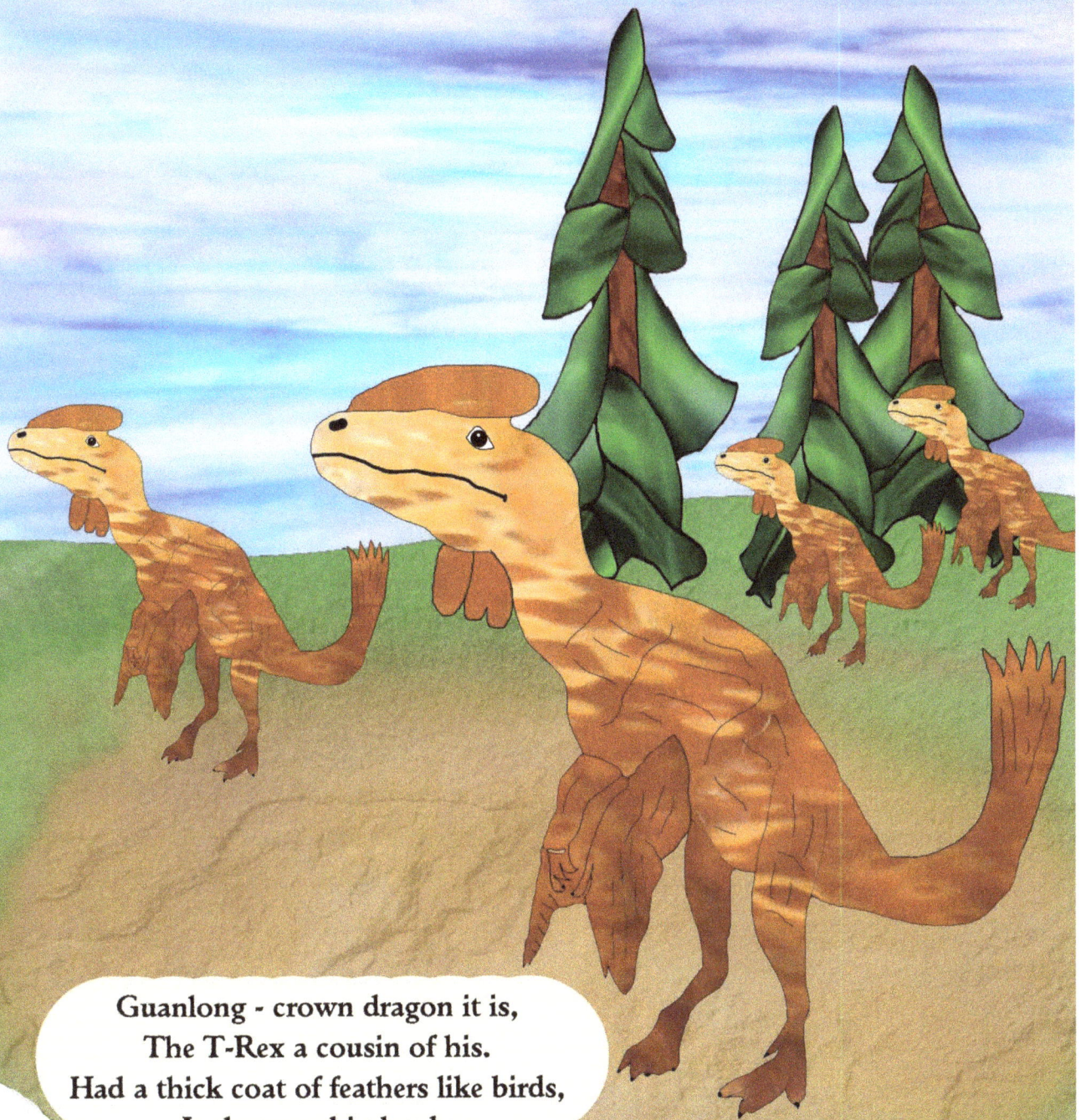

Guanlong - crown dragon it is,
The T-Rex a cousin of his.
Had a thick coat of feathers like birds,
And roamed in herds.

Going to the Cretaceous Period

65 to 146 million years ago

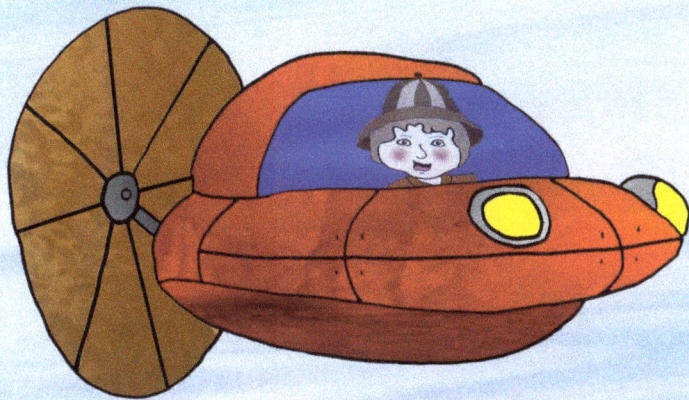

World of the dinosaurs - let's go see,
In Mr. McDoogle's fancy time
machine - Wee!
65 million years we go,
Back to the ages of long ago.

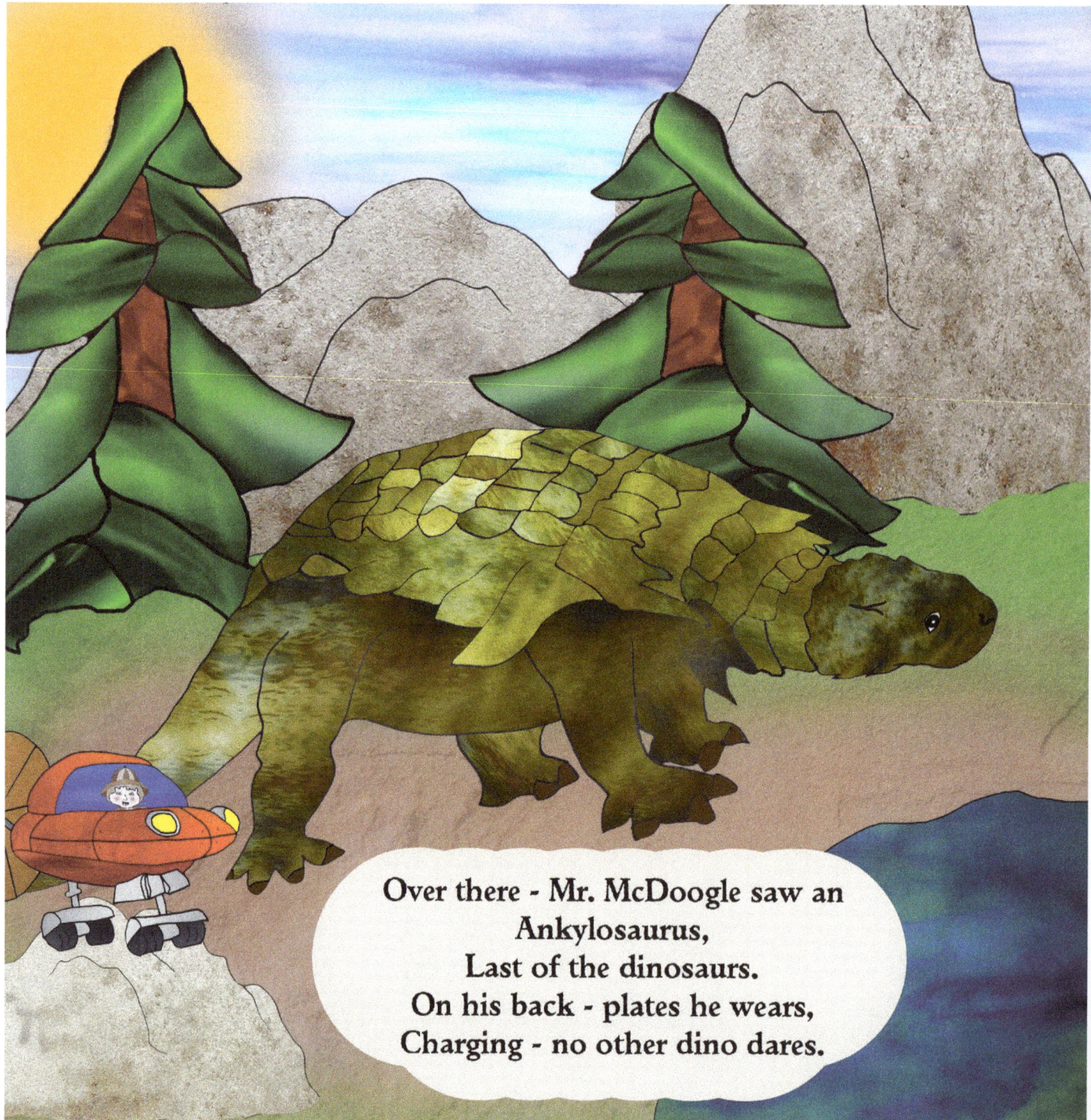

Over there - Mr. McDoogle saw an
Ankylosaurus,
Last of the dinosaurs.
On his back - plates he wears,
Charging - no other dino dares.

Velociraptor - means "speedy thief,"
Caused other dino's grief,
Ran up to 40 mph in a short burst,
Wanted to see who will be first.

Triceratops - had three horns,
To his enemies he warns.
Had 800 teeth - plants he would eat,
That was his treat.

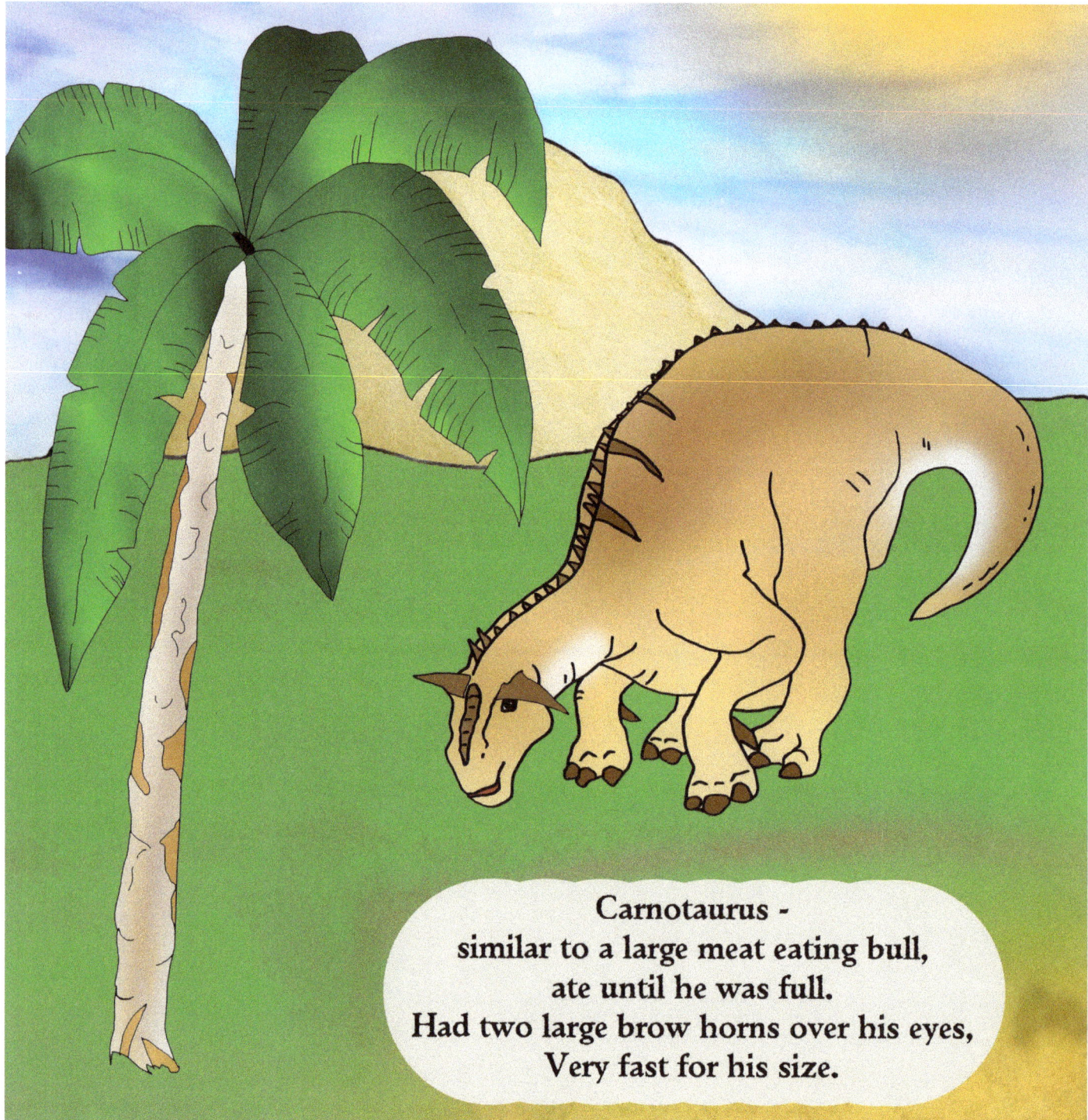

Carnotaurus -
similar to a large meat eating bull,
ate until he was full.
Had two large brow horns over his eyes,
Very fast for his size.

Caulkicephalus - a flying reptile,
Mr. McDoogle watched for a while.
As a person he is tall,
Out of the sky - he would not fall.
With his large teeth he would take,
The fish from the lake.

Rapator - were 30 feet tall,
Listen to them squall.
They will run in packs,
And leave lots of tracks.

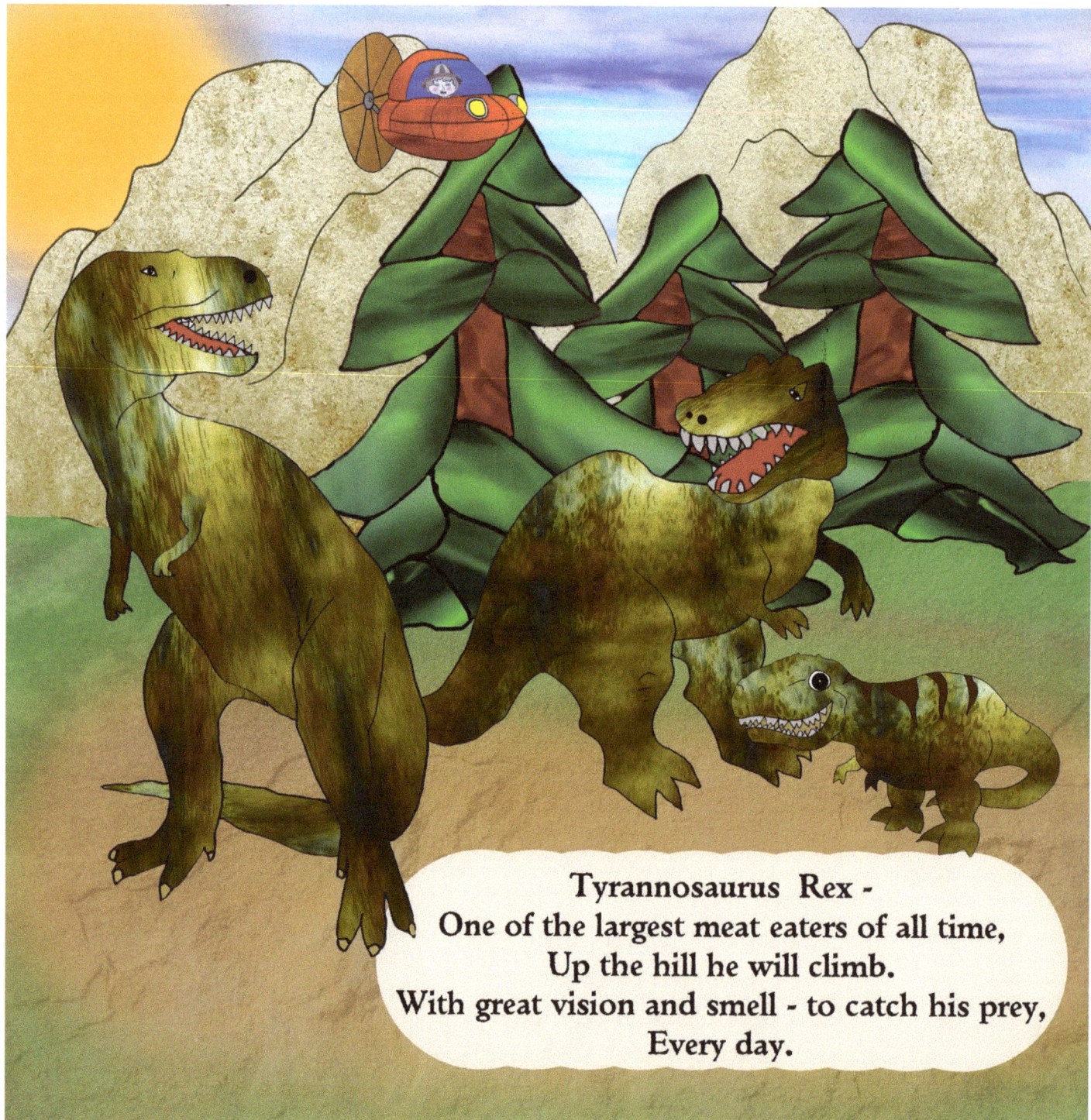

Tyrannosaurus Rex -
One of the largest meat eaters of all time,
Up the hill he will climb.
With great vision and smell - to catch his prey,
Every day.

Agujaceratops -
The woods he lived in,
He was not thin.
Had horns and frills on his head,
The other animals fled.

Time to go back home

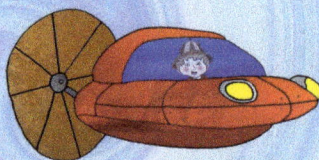

It was fun to roam.

What a beautiful day to take a trip,
Mr. McDoogle did have to zip.
Dinosaurs lived - we saw where,
Exciting to be there.

www.ingramcontent.com/pod-product-compliance
Lightning Source LLC
Chambersburg PA
CBHW060752150426
42811CB00058B/1388